ER 636.1 OBR
)'Brien, Kim,
Friesian horse / by Kim
)'Brien.

D0856576

Horses

Friesian
Horses

by Kim O'Brien

Consulting Editor: Gail Saunders-Smith, PhD

Capstone
press

Mankato, Minnesota

FOUNTAINDALE PUBLIC LIBRARY DISTRICT
300 West Briarcliff Road
Bolingbrook, IL 60440-2894
(630) 759-2102

Pebble Books are published by Capstone Press,
151 Good Counsel Drive, P.O. Box 669, Mankato, Minnesota 56002.
www.capstonepress.com

Copyright © 2010 by Capstone Press, a Capstone Publishers company.
All rights reserved.
No part of this publication may be reproduced in whole or in part, or
stored in a retrieval system, or transmitted in any form or by any means,
electronic, mechanical, photocopying, recording, or otherwise, without
written permission of the publisher.
For information regarding permission, write to Capstone Press,
151 Good Counsel Drive, P.O. Box 669, Dept. R, Mankato, Minnesota 56002.
Printed in the United States of America

Books published by Capstone Press are manufactured with paper
containing at least 10 percent post-consumer waste.

Library of Congress Cataloging-in-Publication Data
O'Brien, Kim, 1960–
    Friesian horses / by Kim O'Brien.
    p. cm. — (Pebble books. Horses.)
    Includes bibliographical references and index.
    Summary: "A brief introduction to the characteristics, life cycle, and uses of the
Friesian horse breed" — Provided by publisher.
    ISBN-13: 978-1-4296-3304-8 (library binding)
    1. Friesian horse — Juvenile literature. I. Title. II. Series.
SF293.F9O27 2010
636.1 — dc22   2008048888

Note to Parents and Teachers

The Horses set supports national science standards related to life
science. This book describes and illustrates the Friesian horse.
The images support early readers in understanding the text.
The repetition of words and phrases helps early readers learn
new words. This book also introduces early readers to
subject-specific vocabulary words, which are defined in the
Glossary section. Early readers may need assistance to read some
words and to use the Table of Contents, Glossary, Read More,
Internet Sites, and Index sections of the book.

Table of Contents

Fancy Friesians

Friesian horses have black coats.

Friesians are calm horses with a kind nature.

Friesians have thick manes and long, flowing tails. This powerful breed carries its head high.

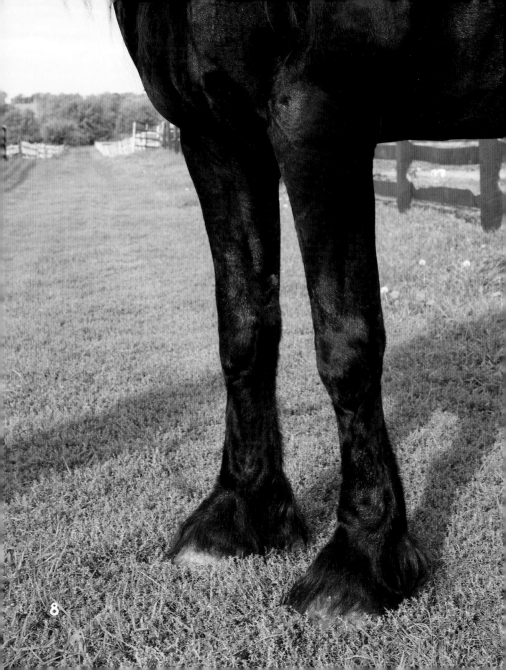

8

Friesians have long hair
on their legs.
This hair is called feathers.

Friesians have big bones
and muscular bodies.
They lift their legs high
when they gallop.

From Foal to Adult

Friesian foals are born
with light coats.
Their coats become all black
after one year.

withers

Adult Friesians stand
15 to 16 hands tall.
They weigh about
1,500 pounds
(680 kilograms).

Horses are measured in hands.
Each hand is 4 inches (10 centimeters).
A horse is measured from the ground
to its withers.

15

Strong Horses

Friesians are

good dressage horses.

Friesians show off their

powerful bodies in dressage.

18

Teams of Friesians
perform drills.
They step together.

Friesians are smart,
gentle horses.
They even bow
and do other tricks.

Glossary

bow — to bend over

breed — a group of animals that come from common relatives

dressage — the art of guiding a horse through different movements

drill — to perform a movement over and over again

foal — a young horse

gallop — to run quickly with all four feet leaving the ground at one time

mane — the long, thick hair that grows on the head and neck of some animals, such as horses and ponies

nature — an animal's personality

team — two or more horses that work together

Read More

Kama Einhorn. *My First Book about Horses and Ponies.*
New York: Random House, 2008.

Pitts, Zachary. *The Pebble First Guide to Horses.*
First Guides. Mankato, Minn.: Capstone Press, 2009.

Internet Sites

FactHound offers a safe, fun way to find Internet sites
related to this book. All of the sites on FactHound have been
researched by our staff.

Here's all you do:

Visit *www.facthound.com*

FactHound will fetch the best sites for you!

Index

Word Count: 118

Grade: 1

Early-Intervention Level: 18

Editorial Credits

Sarah L. Schuette, editor; Bobbi J. Wyss, designer

Photo Credits

Capstone Press/TJ Thoraldson Digital Photography, cover, 1, 4, 6, 8, 10, 12, 14, 20
Mon Cheval/Tony Brack, 16, 18

The author dedicates this book in memory of her grandmother, Katherine
Boulware Sutton.